Angels

Helping Us

Contend

Greg Crawford

Published by:

Creative Release Publishing

Des Moines, Iowa

thebaseiowa.org

Printed in the United States

First printing 2009

ISBN – 978-1481928465

Contents

Introduction

With so many in this hour being focused upon the supernatural and its workings, I, too, went on a journey and told God "I need to know about the unseen realm and how it works". This teaching is the result of what God revealed to me about the unseen realm. In all honesty, I was quite shocked about how far away from the truth our understanding is concerning angels. Even today, many pastors, especially evangelicals, are proclaiming things about angels that are not doctrinally correct. I looked into many sources of information that could be connected doctrinally and not just visitations people experienced. This book is a doctrinal handbook concerning angels and I show the governmental structure God has for them as well and how it inter-acts with us.

Greg Crawford

1

Angelic Visitations

Many of us hear differing opinions concerning angels. There are many books that have been written on them. Most of these come from the perspective of trying to bring understanding based entirely upon experience without any doctrinal proof to back up what is being said. I believe that we are all having visitations with angels. Some we are aware of, but most of the time, we are very much unaware.

During the Christmas season is when we seem to hear the most about angels. We sing songs about them, read the Christmas story, see the displays of angels overlooking manger scenes in churchyards. But yet there is much more than the fantasy and imagination of the mind that these images conjure up. Angels have been divinely positioned to help us contend for the advancement of the Kingdom upon the Earth. God sends Angels into our life to bring us messages, confront our hearts, and also to war for us in the unseen realm.

I have had many angelic visitations but have been unaware of exactly the reasoning behind where the working of what each one of these meant. With the New Age cult emerging and bringing forth angels of light, we, as God's people, must have a clear understanding of the true angelic hosts of the Lord of Lords and King of Kings. If we do not understand the government of angels, their positions and functions, we, too will be deceived to embrace angels of light that will lead us astray.

We have recently seen this with some of the well-known evangelists bringing revival into America, specifically embracing an angel named Emma. As the revival was unfolding in Florida and Todd Bentley was announcing this visitation with this angel on an ongoing basis, I decided to look further into it to gain understanding.

What I found was very alarming and also very disturbing. The angel Emma was a real angel recognized in Japanese occultism. How Todd Bentley had described this angel was exactly how those in the occult describe the angel as well. Even the very name of that angel was the name that they had used. That is what first led me into the understanding about angels of light. Others have seen and talked with this angel as well. But the outcome seems to be the same, there really is no Kingdom advancement or fruit produced that is lasting from these encounters.

But, what I did see was a major distraction in the Body of Christ trying to entertain angels, call upon angels, and in one case, I heard of a woman who received a healing from an angel when there is no Biblical precedent for angels bringing healing. In this case, the woman's healing lasted only about a week but the public testimony of it caused many to seek after that same angel of healing. I know of someone in the occult who was casting out demons using Jesus' Name but yet, they were not a believer. They were charging $500 for every deliverance. They understood the power of the Name of Jesus yet they did not want to submit to the Lordship. What happened in these people's lives was they were deceived and believing they were delivered. The reality is they got relief for a season of roughly 6 months but then the demons manifested again in their life. So what the people did was come back to receive another deliverance. This is the kind of things that angels of light do to distract from true freedom to bring a freedom that lasts for a short season which causes greater bondage at the end.

Without a solid Biblical understanding of the things in the spiritual realm, we can be easily led astray. People can be talked into seeing things, hearing things and even experiencing things that did not come from God but came from their own imagination and fantasy. As a culture today that is based so much on the fantasy of what the mind can imagine, we have to be sure that we are not allowing the imaginations of our mind to create something that is not truly there or from God.

I will share a couple experiences that I have had with angels to hopefully help us understand how these angels truly work.

Several years ago I was traveling back from a meeting across the state. It was late at night and I saw a man hitchhiking along the side of the road. I was debating about stopping as I saw him appearing in my headlights. I went by quite a ways before I finally got the car completely stopped and I backed up to pick up this young man. We got in the car and started a conversation that seemed very simple yet seemed to carry a lot of weight in the words being said. I asked him if he was a Christian and he would not give me a solid answer. It was as if he was avoiding the answer yet I had a sense of the presence of God resting upon his life. We rode together for about 20 min. talking about the things of God and what God was doing in that moment in the Earth.

When it was time to let him out, he said "You could just pull over to the side of the road here". There was a small grouping of houses sitting across the creek with a pretty short driveway to them. He said "you don't have to pull in, I'll just walk". I asked him if this is where he lived and he replied "yes, this is where I'm at". I told him I wouldn't just let him off along the side of the road but asked him to show me which house to be dropped off at. He said "that one right there". It was late at night so I said "I will make sure you can get inside the door". It appeared as if it had been left unlocked for him but there were no lights on. He went through the door and the porch light came on inside. I drove off feeling somewhat dazed and wondering if I just encountered an angel. The conversation was sure focused on God, yet it seemed as if I didn't learn any new insights about God. I thought on it for several days and finally kind of dismissed it.

About two weeks later, I was back on that same road driving by where I dropped this man off. I decided maybe I'll stop and see if he is home then I can have another conversation with him. I pulled in the driveway, drove up to the house and got out and walked up to the front door. I knocked on the door and an old man and woman came to the door. I said "I'm here to see the young man that lives here". They said "Well, there is no young man that lives here. We have lived here our entire lives. I said "I dropped him off a couple weeks ago. Did you have a visitor?" They said "No, we've not had any visitors and nobody has stopped by that is a young man like you're describing".

I walked away now really beginning to realize that I had an encounter with an Angel. I began to piece together that God was trying to show me that the spiritual realm was more real than the natural realm. He was also trying to show me that there was an angel assigned to this older couple to look after them. From that point, I started becoming more aware that there are indeed angels around all the time.

Another time I experienced an angelic visitation that was not just me in the room but many others. We were in the midst of a meeting in Waterloo, Iowa. We'd been traveling the state doing awakening meetings trying to stir up the hearts of God's people. The meeting came to a very high point in worship. I started to hear other voices that sounded like women singing louder than the people in the room. I looked up at the stage area and realized that our female singers were not singing. I looked around me and there was nobody singing extremely loud around me at all. The volume started increasing and I noticed others looking around as well. What we were all experiencing was an angelic host had joined in our worship. We had opened a portal into heaven and they were singing with us. When the meeting was over, I asked others if they heard what I had heard. Everyone said the same thing; we have heard the angels sing with us today!

I know several people that God gives them the ability to see angels. People came up to me after preaching and said I saw two angels standing beside you. I know a young boy who could see both demons and angels in rooms. I believe that God gives these opportunities so that we would have an understanding that heaven is real. There's an entire host in heaven of angels that we usually dismiss, deny, or ignore. Once we begin to understand the function of angels, their role or positions, we begin to draw upon a heavenly host that's just waiting for the decree of our words!

Greg Crawford

2

Angelic Functions

Hebrews 1:13-14

13 But to which of the angels said he at any time, Sit on my right hand, until I make thine enemies thy footstool? 14 Are they not all ministering spirits, sent forth to minister for them who shall be heirs of salvation?

Even though all angels have different functions, there are two distinct things they all have in common. First, they exist to serve God. Everything they do has a serving aspect to it. Since Jesus came as a servant of all, his ministers are looked upon as servants and we, as believers, are to be serving humanity. It makes sense that what he has created exists to only serve him.

The second thing all angels have in common is they obey God's intentions. How angels walk this out is not based on what we believe to be the best in a situation, but entirely upon the desires of God's heart. They follow God's plan without deviating from His overall intention. Once we understand these two things, it is easier for us to engage angels in our everyday life.

Looking at two angels' names, Michael and Gabriel, we see the attributes of these two distinct things that all angels have in common.

Michael means "who is like God"

Gabriel means "man of God" or "God has shown Himself strong,"

In function and application these two, especially, display the angel's role as reflecting characteristics of God Himself as a servant. They also reflect the attitude of God's heart in the intention of what He desires.

Yet, as servants of God that should know the intention of God's heart, He places us at a higher role than angels. God believes we know His heart like David did, we are in tune with the season and what His beat is. Yet many of us only understand the workings of God in some of the shallowest of thinking.

1 Corinthians 6:3 Know ye not that we shall judge angels? how much more things that pertain to this life?

If we truly understood the intentions of God's heart, we would be able to rightly divide and judge the things that are happening in this life. From the verse above, we see that it says that we shall judge angels. This is not passing sentence upon their actions but being able to understand that their actions are a reflection of the intention of God's heart. It is like having the gift of discernment to discern what spirit something is or is not. It is also to understand that we are able to see Him peer into their actions and to understand God's intentions.

Hebrews 1:4-7

[4] *Being made so much better than the angels, as he hath by inheritance obtained a more excellent name than they.* [5] *For unto which of the angels said he at any time, Thou art my Son, this day have I begotten thee? And again, I will be to him a Father, and he shall be to me a Son?* [6] *And again, when he bringeth in the firstbegotten into the world, he*

saith, And let all the angels of God worship him. [7] And of the angels he saith, Who maketh his angels spirits, and his ministers a flame of fire.

We need to clearly understand the working of angels and the working of the Holy Spirit. This, as well, gets us into trouble. We sometimes give credit to angels when in reality there is no legal way they are allowed to do what we think they can. Both are spirit beings but they function very differently. Angels have come from the creative outflow of God. But the Holy Spirit is actually part of the Deity and part of the creative source of God.

- The Holy Spirit manifests the nature of God.
- Angels manifest the intentions of God.

- The Holy Spirit brings the source of all life.
- Angels bring according to what is sovereign or what God has determined.

- The Holy Spirit brings the nature of God.
- Angels are God's agents of providence.

If we look at these in the simplest form when we draw upon the nature of God, and the source of all life, we see the nature of God manifest through the Holy Spirit.

When we draw upon the intentions of God and what God has already determined, and realize that God has agents of providence bringing those intentions to the Earth, we start putting a demand upon angelic hosts.

You see, when we finally reach out in faith it puts a determination of God into motion, thus releasing angels. Faith also puts the nature of God into motion thus releasing the Holy Spirit to form or produce God's nature within us and around us. Thus our faith is released towards God's determination and the Holy Spirit with the nature of God. Angels are then set into motion to engage in the affairs of God and the intentions on the Earth. When we hit those same intentions, then we have angels at our disposal. But angels are not at our disposal for common things unrelated to the Kingdom of God.

Angels have certain limitations that we need to be aware of. Angels cannot create, they cannot change substances, they cannot alter the laws of nature, they cannot perform miracles, they cannot act without means, and they cannot search the heart. They may know the intentions of our heart because it has been revealed to them by God. God allows this so angels can act on the minds of men. They can do this by acting on God's intentions through outward actions that affect how we perceive situations, events and responses. They have to operate within spiritual boundaries.

They do not act by direct operation upon the mind, which is the peculiar prerogative of God and His Spirit, but by the suggestion of truth and guidance of thought and feeling, much as one man may act upon another.

The power of angels is, therefore:

(1.) Dependent and received from a source

(2.) It must be exercised in accordance with the laws of the material and spiritual world.

 (3.) Their intervention is not optional, but permitted or commanded by God at His pleasure and so far as the external world is concerned, it would seem to be only occasional and exceptional.

These limitations are of the greatest practical importance. We are not to regard angels as intervening between us and God, or to attribute to them the effects which the Bible everywhere refers to the providential agency of God. Nor should we credit them with what the Holy Spirit has actually done. All of these types of wrong responses bring us into the worshipping of angels. Angel worship is forbidden by God and aligns itself with Satan worship as Satan was a heavenly angel at one time.

The Scriptures teach that the holy angels are employed;

(1.) In the worship of God.
- We see continuous worship before the throne by certain angelic host.
- We see all angels approaching the throne.
- They all approached in the posture of giving worship to God.
- We approach mostly in a posture of taking from God.

(2.) In executing the will of God.

- In the Old Testament, angels appeared to reveal the will of God.
- Since we have the Holy Spirit and the Spirit's witness in the New Testament, they come to aid in the implementation of God's will.

(3.) And especially in ministering to the heirs of salvation.

- **Matthew 18:10** we see them watching over infants
- **Psalm 34:7** we see them aiding those who are mature in age
- **Luke 16:22** we see them with those who are dying
- We see them from the start of life to the finish of life involved in humanity.

3

Categories of Angels

Hebrews 13:2

² *Be not forgetful to entertain strangers: for thereby some have entertained angels unawares.*

Angels are spirit beings. Although angels may reveal themselves to mankind in the form of human bodies, they nonetheless are called "spirits" suggesting they do not have resemblance to natural bodies. Hence, they do not function as human beings in terms of marriage (**Mark 12:25**) nor are they subject to death (**Luke 20:36**).

Angels sometimes have a spiritual makeup that makes them appear in a human form. I believe God does this so it is easier for us to receive and relate. Unlike Jessie Duplantis saw in a vision, angels do not reproduce other angels as they are created beings (**Matt. 22:30**).

Since they are spiritual beings they are under spiritual law. Once we truly get a firm grip on spiritual law, it allows us to see how angels begin to play a role in the Kingdom advance on the earth.

Luke 20:35-36 But they which shall be accounted worthy to obtain that world, and the resurrection from the dead, neither marry, nor are given in marriage : 36 Neither can they die any more: for they are equal unto the angels; and are the children of God, being the children of the resurrection.

The scripture is clear, angels do not die and they are created beings. This means from the beginning of time, they have always been after God created them. We call them eternal beings when in reality they are everlasting beings.

We, on the other hand, are eternal beings. We receive eternal life. It is life that has always been as it is everlasting, but for us, it is eternal from the point of salvation forward, meaning it has no end. What is everlasting has an untraceable beginning.

The reason we call angels created beings is David called for all nature to praise God for His creation. It is a call for creation to call forth praise. Since angels are created, we automatically call them created beings. This is true but is not their current state. It is the event of life for them. All things are actually created, which means there was a point of life springing forth where there was no life. Not only are angels everlasting, but we know God created them. We see in scripture the day they came into existence. So they are created, everlasting and eternal.

Along with the celestial bodies, the Lord created the angels by His word. **(Ps. 148:2–5)** Job was reminded that the angels sang praise to God when they were created. **(Job 38:6–7)** Christ created the angels that they might ultimately give praise to Him. **(Col. 1:16)**.

Angels were created before the earth was created. God's original intention was the angels would be created for service to Him. Now imagine this that God has allowed angels to be at our disposal as well. That is a high degree of honor that God shows towards us.

Since they were created before the earth, this enabled God to have a group that would cheer and rejoice at what He would create. It is like the angels ooh-ed and aah-ed at what God had done. **Job 38:6** says they did this with great shouts of joy at creation. Now imagine when God created another created being; man, to have fellowship with Him. Angels created to serve Him, but man created for fellowship. This is a greater positioning. Imagine how the angels must have rejoiced over this! Yes, we are higher than the angels!

We have touched on angels at a higher order than man, but man is placed above them positioned for relationship with God. Mankind, including our incarnate Lord, is "lower than the angels" according to **Heb. 2:7.** Angels are not subject to the limitations of man, especially since they are incapable of death (**Luke 20:36**). Angels, however, have limitations compared to man, particularly in future relationships. Angels are not created in the image of God, therefore, they do not share man's glorious destiny of redemption in Christ. This alone puts man at a higher position than angels. At the consummation of the age, redeemed man will be exalted above angels.

1 Corinthians 6:3 (KJV 1900) — 3 Know ye not that we shall judge angels? how much more things that pertain to this life?

But the scripture tells us in **2 Sam 14:20** that angels have wisdom that man can attain to, yet it is limited wisdom. It comes from God but is not the totality of God's wisdom. They have access into this wisdom much like we do on a 'need to know' basis. But remember the 'need to know' for angels is to do service for God and our 'need to know' is because of our relationship with God. So angels do not know all things, but we have the ability one day to know Him as He is!

Angels seem to be less restricted because they are 100% spiritual beings without bodies being restricted in movement. But they are limited in how much power they can move in. They did remove the stone from the tomb but they were serving the intentions of God.

But humanity once connected to the unlimited possibilities of God, will do more than roll a stone away. This is another aspect angels desire to look into that we have. I imagine they must wonder why we don't exercise this power more often and why our spiritual senses are so dull in not knowing the intentions of God.

Colossians 1:16 (KJV 1900) — 16 For by him were all things created, that are in heaven, and that are in earth, visible and invisible, whether they be thrones, or dominions, or principalities, or powers: all things were created by him, and for him:

Angels were created simultaneously and innumerable in number. The statement of creation in **Colossians 1:16** points to the creation of angels as a singular act; the act of creating angels does not continue, nor does God continue to create more angels as the Bible unfolds. Because the angels are incapable of reproducing, their number remains constant. It does not increase nor decrease. The number of their creation is "myriads" according to **Heb 12:22** … "an innumerable company of angels" The term 'innumerable' is the Greek word *myraids* (Gk. *muriasin*). It literally means ten thousand; here it denotes "countless thousands". This same description is seen again in **Rev. 5:11**. The repetition of myriads in **Revelation 5:11** suggests the number of angels is countless. In other words, it is a number so large we are not able to count, but it is not a number that is endless.

But this does not mean God could not or has not created more angels, just the angels we read of and assume exist may not be the only ones in existence or ever will be in existence. Perhaps once there is a new heavens and Earth and we begin to truly rule and reign over … galaxies, planets, other new created beings, etc., then the need for more angelic host might justify God releasing His creative ability again and enlarging the angelic host.

4

Fallen Angels

Ephesians 6:12 (KJV 1900) — 12 For we wrestle not against flesh and blood, but against principalities, against powers, against the rulers of the darkness of this world, against spiritual wickedness in high places.

As we begin now to look further into the different groupings of angels, we will start out with a simple classification structure found in **Ephesians 6:12**. This ranking we all know is a ranking of fallen angels. Looking at the definitions of the words enables us to further understand that God has an order to all things even fallen angels.

rulers are "those who are first or high in rank"
powers are "those invested with authority"

rulers of darkness "expresses the power or authority which they exercise over the world" This includes cults and occult practices.

spiritual wickedness describes the wicked spirits, "expressing their character and nature" This is the sin nature.

Now I don't want to put emphasis on fallen angels, but I do want us to gain understanding in this area before we see the depth of all the rest of the angels and the overall workings of God on our behalf.

The Devils Fall

Isaiah 14:12 How art thou fallen from heaven, O Lucifer, son of the morning! how art thou cut down to the ground, which didst weaken the nations!

Isaiah 14:13-15) For thou hast said in thine heart, I will ascend into heaven, I will exalt my throne above the stars of God: I will sit also upon the mount of the congregation, in the sides of the north: I will ascend above the heights of the clouds; I will be like the most High.

Isaiah 14:15-20   Yet thou shalt be brought down to hell, to the sides of the pit. They that see thee shall narrowly look upon thee, and consider thee, saying, Is this the man that made the earth to tremble, that did shake kingdoms; That made the world as a wilderness, and destroyed the cities thereof; that opened not the house of his prisoners? All the kings of the nations, even all of them, lie in glory, every one in his own house. But thou art cast out of thy grave like an abominable branch, and as the raiment of those that are slain, thrust through with a sword, that go down to the stones of the pit; as a carcase trodden under feet. Thou shalt not be joined with them in burial, because thou hast destroyed thy land, and slain thy people: the seed of evildoers shall never be renowned.

Ezek 28:14 KJV

Thou art the anointed cherub that covereth; and I have set thee so: thou wast upon the holy mountain of God; thou hast walked up and down in the midst of the stones of fire. Thou wast perfect in thy ways from the day that thou wast created, till iniquity was found in thee. By the multitude of thy merchandise they have filled the midst of thee with violence, and thou hast sinned: therefore I will cast thee as profane out of the mountain of God: and I will destroy thee, O covering cherub, from the midst of the stones of fire.

Notice all that he had. He had all rights and access to God. But he had one thing he shouldn't have, he had pride. It was found in him. God is the maker of all things. He has even made pride. But anything in

excess becomes iniquity or twisted thinking. So
God cast him to the ground or expelled him from
heaven. He placed him on Earth so man could rule
over him.

Ezek 28:17-19 KJV

*Thine heart was lifted up because of thy beauty,
thou hast corrupted thy wisdom by reason of thy
brightness: I will cast thee to the ground, I will lay
thee before kings, that they may behold thee. Thou
hast defiled thy sanctuaries by the multitude of
thine iniquities, by the iniquity of thy traffic;
therefore will I bring forth a fire from the midst of
thee, it shall devour thee, and I will bring thee to
ashes upon the earth in the sight of all them that
behold thee. All they that know thee among the
people shall be astonished at thee: thou shalt be a
terror, and never shalt thou be any more.*

Basically the devil is not equal to God, nor does he
have a kingdom, so we are not fighting kingdom
against kingdom. He is only an angel and a fallen
angel, at that. The only authority he has is what
mankind gives him as he has no delegated
authority from God.

Origin of Demons

There was no sin in heaven nor was there a major corruption or over throw of a third of the angels in heaven. Only the devil fell. This interpretation of angelic activity in heaven is completely false. Even Jesus said "I see Satan falling from heaven as lightening". He never references any other angels. The desire of Satan to be like God became sin when he acted it out in the deception to Adam and Eve. Iniquity is the thought, sin is the action. Satan had iniquity in heaven but could not sin or bring it to action in heaven. But the iniquity alone was enough for him to be removed from heaven.

So after he was cast out of heaven, he then acted out the iniquity and produced sin in the earth, for until the deception, the earth was sinless. He then became the "principle" or first in rank. He was the first in rank of iniquity, sin and transgression.

But what about the other angels? God had placed them here in the earth as angels to help man rule Earth. They were called "watchers" and Daniel spoke of them as well as other sources. These fallen angels were originally called the watchers who came to the earth.

Now, to discuss the deception. Because of sin upon the earth, it was so far reaching once released that it had an effect on the angels and they became corrupted.

These are the angels that fell while here upon the earth in a sin environment. That is how far reaching sin was. It shows how far reaching our redemption is as well.

These fallen angels became powers or ones with designated authority. I believe you could say they were empowered with authority which they have no option but to follow.

2 Peter 2:4 For if God spared not the angels that sinned, but cast them down to hell, and delivered them into chains of darkness, to be reserved unto judgment;

These angels are held in a place until a time of judgment for their actions. They are held from several things, but have free reign until that time of judgment happens.

Jude 6 And the angels which kept not their first estate, but left their own habitation, he hath reserved in everlasting chains under darkness unto the judgment of the great day.

These same angels are seen here leaving their first estate and habitation. This is talking about them violating God's order and purpose for them. The translation actually states they are denied access back into heaven. You see, they did not sin, there was not a coup. They did have access and something happened to them that denied them that access!

The Bible tells us the angels desire to look into the things we have access to. We tend to only think of the angels in heaven. The reality is the fallen angels wish they could participate "in such a great redemption". We have the things they once had, God's attention, access, privilege, etc. Perhaps the verse is pointing more towards the fallen angels than the heavenly ones so we would value our redemption even more!

Demons are not angels

So we have laid this teaching out this way to come to a conclusion and that is demons are not angels but are actually offspring of fallen angels. This offspring has a historically documented origin. Enoch is probably one of the best kept secrets most Christians have never heard of. This book is not canonized scripture, but is looked at as such by the Ethiopian Jews. The devil has hidden this book from the Church because in it holds some answers to the spiritual battle we now fight.

The Bible is the inspired word of God, but could there be more inspired Word that is just not canonized? Enoch wrote this book down as a historical document for the next generations. Now let me tell you that Jesus quoted Enoch and the book of Jubilees, so did Paul, and when we read the New Testament, we are reading sections from both of these books!

Genesis 5:18-24

18 And Jared lived an hundred sixty and two years, and he begat Enoch : 19 And Jared lived after he begat Enoch eight hundred years, and begat sons and daughters : 20 And all the days of Jared were nine hundred sixty and two years: *and he died .*

21 And Enoch lived sixty and five years, and begat Methuselah : 22 And Enoch walked with God after he begat Methuselah three hundred years, and begat sons and daughters : 23 And all the days of Enoch were three hundred sixty and five years : 24 And Enoch walked with God: and he was not; for God took him.

Hebrews 11:5

5 By faith Enoch was translated that he should not see death; and was not found, because God had translated him: for before his translation he had this testimony, that he pleased God.

Jude 14

14 And Enoch also, the seventh from Adam, prophesied of these, saying, Behold, the Lord cometh with ten thousands of his saints,

Before Enoch was no more because God took him, God allowed him to peer into the heavens and showed him the working of all things. Enoch was able to record these things in detail. We will look at this somewhat as much detail is given to angelic activity.

The Genesis dilemma

Genesis 6:2 That the sons of God saw the daughters of men that they were fair; and they took them wives of all which they chose.

This statement has always been hard for theologians to explain and generally is avoided.

Genesis 6:4 There were giants in the earth in those days; and also after that, when the sons of God came in unto the daughters of men, and they bare children to them, the same became mighty men which were of old, men of renown.

The word Giant means "Nephilim"= fall, cast down violently, fall away. We see a type of this word used in the description of the spirit of the giants in:

Enoch 15:9-10

⁹The spirits of the giants shall be like clouds, ⁽²⁵⁾ which shall oppress, corrupt, fall, content, and bruise upon earth.

(25) <u>The Greek word for "clouds" here, nephelas, may disguise a more ancient reading, Napheleim (Nephilim).</u>

¹⁰They shall cause lamentation. <u>No food shall they eat; and they shall be thirsty; they shall be concealed, and shall not ⁽²⁶⁾ rise up against the sons of men, and against women; for they come forth during the days of slaughter and destruction.</u>

The giants that were produced came from the result of watcher angels looking at the women of the earth and took them as wives. The words 'sons of God' often referred to angels and God's created beings. Within two verses from **Gen. 6:2- Gen. 6:4,** we have giants on the earth.

Another book that is looked at is the book of Jubilees. This book, like the book of Enoch, is also being considered as possible canonized scripture. Here Gen. 6:4 is referenced again. But this time, it is more defined. Specifically, it says the angels mated with the wives and the result was giants!

Jubilee [Chapter 5]

1 And it came to pass when the children of men began to multiply on the face of the earth and daughters were born unto them, that the angels of God saw them on a certain year of this jubilee, that they were beautiful to look upon; and they took themselves wives of all whom they 2 chose, and they bare unto them sons and they were giants. And lawlessness increased on the earth and all flesh corrupted its way, alike men and cattle and beasts and birds and everything that walks on the earth -all of them corrupted their ways and their orders, and they began to devour each other, and lawlessness increased on the earth and every imagination of the thoughts of all men

The book of Giants, another reference, also speaks of 200 angels who became corrupted and mated with the women of the earth. The offspring were 450 feet high.

Enoch 16:1

And as to the death of the giants, wheresoever their spirits depart from their bodies, let their flesh, that which is perishable, be without judgment. (27) **Thus shall they perish, until the day of the great consummation of the great world. A destruction shall take place of the Watchers and the impious.**

What is this great destruction talked about? Is it in scripture? Yes, it is the flood!

During this time, all of mankind was destroyed off the face of the earth as God was wroth with man. This destroyed all unrighteous people and the giants that were the offspring of man. What would happen to an offspring from an angel and a woman? They could not go to heaven as they are sinful. They could not go to hell as it is designed for un-renewed fallen man after judgment. The conclusion is:

We have spirit beings loose who, at one time, were used to inhabiting a body upon the face of the earth, indulging in all sinful pleasures, but now has no body to inhabit. These are the demons or evil spirits that we fight today. They are seeking places of habitation once again.

Jubilees and Enoch both say as the Bible does, they are in a dry and arid place.

Luke 11:24-26

24 *When the unclean spirit is gone out of a man, he walketh through dry places, seeking rest; and finding none, he saith, I will return unto my house whence I came out.* **25** *And when he cometh, he findeth it swept and garnished.* **26** *Then goeth he, and taketh to him seven other spirits more wicked than himself; and they enter in, and dwell there: and the last state of that man is worse than the first.*

Matthew 12:43 *When the unclean spirit is gone out of a man, he walketh through dry places, seeking rest, and findeth none.*

Offspring of The Watchers

If the Watchers mated with the women of the earth, the result was a mutant type race that was half human and half spirit being. The book of Jubilee confirms this.

Jubilee 10:5-7

5 And Thou knowest how Thy Watchers, the fathers of these spirits, acted in my day: and as for these *spirits which are living, imprison them and hold them fast in the place of condemnation, and let them not bring destruction on the sons of thy servant, my God; for these are malignant, and 6 created in order to destroy. And let them <u>not rule over the spirits of the living</u>; for Thou alone canst exercise dominion over them. And let them not have power over the sons of the righteous 7 from henceforth and for evermore.' And the Lord our God bade us to bind all. And the chief of the spirits, Mastema, came and said: '<u>Lord, Creator, let some of them remain before me, and let them harken to my voice, and do all that I shall say unto them; for if some of them are not left to me, I shall not be able to execute the power of my will on the sons of men</u>; for these are for corruption and leading astray before my judgment, for great is the wickedness of the sons of men.'*

Jesus quoted the book of Enoch

Enoch Chapter 15

[1]*Then addressing me, He spoke and said, Hear, neither be afraid, O righteous Enoch<u>, you scribe of righteousness</u>: approach hither, and hear my voice. Go, say <u>to the Watchers of heaven, who have sent you to pray for them, You ought to pray for men, and not men for you.</u>*

[2]*Wherefore have you forsaken the lofty and holy*

45

heaven, which endures for ever, and have lain with women; have defile yourselves with the daughters of men; have taken to yourselves wives; have acted like the sons of the earth, and have begotten an impious offspring? [23]

(23) An impious offspring. Literally, "giants" (Charles, p. 82; Knibb, p. 101).

³You being spiritual, holy, and possessing a life which is eternal, have polluted yourselves with women; have begotten in carnal blood; have lusted in the blood of men; and have done as those who are flesh and blood do.

⁴These however die and perish.

⁵Therefore have I given to them wives, that they might cohabit with them; that sons might be born of them; and that this might be transacted upon earth.

⁶But you from the beginning were made spiritual, possessing a life which is eternal, and not subject to death for ever.

⁷Therefore I made not wives for you, because, being spiritual, your dwelling is in heaven.

⁸Now the giants, who have been born of spirit and of flesh, shall be called upon earth evil spirits, and on earth shall be their habitation. Evil spirits shall proceed from their flesh, because they were created

from above; from the holy Watchers was their beginning and primary foundation. Evil spirits shall they be upon earth, and the spirits of the wicked shall they be called. The habitation of the spirits of heaven shall be in heaven; but upon earth shall be the habitation of terrestrial spirits, who are born on earth. (24)

(24) Note the many implications of verses 3-8 regarding the progeny of evil spirits.

⁹*The spirits of the giants shall be like clouds,* (25) *which shall oppress, corrupt, fall, content, and bruise upon earth.*

(25) The Greek word for "clouds" here, nephelas, may disguise a more ancient reading, Napheleim (Nephilim).

¹⁰*They shall cause lamentation. No food shall they eat; and they shall be thirsty; they shall be concealed, and shall not* (26) *rise up against the sons of men, and against women; for they come forth during the days of slaughter and destruction.*

Enoch Chapter 10

¹*Then the Most High, the Great and Holy One spoke,*²*And sent Arsayalalyur* (12) *to the son of Lamech,(12) Arsayalalyur. Here one Greek text reads "Uriel."*³*Saying, Say to him in my name,*

Conceal yourself.[4]*Then explain to him the consummation which is about to take place; for all the earth shall perish; the waters of a deluge shall come over the whole earth, and all things which are in it shall be destroyed.*

[5]*And now teach him how he may escape, and how his seed may remain in all the earth.*

[6]*Again the Lord said to Raphael, Bind Azazyel hand and foot; cast him into darkness; and opening the desert which is in Dudael, cast him in there.*

[7]*Throw upon him hurled and pointed stones, covering him with darkness;*

[8]*There shall he remain for ever; cover his face, that he may not see the light.*

[9]*And in the great day of judgment let him be cast into the fire.*

[10]*Restore the earth, which the angels have corrupted; and announce life to it, that I may revive it.*

[11]*All the sons of men shall not perish in consequence of every secret, by which the Watchers have destroyed, and which they have taught, their offspring.*

[12]*All the earth has been corrupted by the effects of the teaching of Azazyel. To him therefore ascribe*

the whole crime.

What are watchers?

Daniel called an angel a "watcher". This is a type of angel that they distinguished from other angels.

Daniel 4:13 I saw in the visions of my head upon my bed, and, behold, a watcher and an holy one came down from heaven;

Daniel also realized that there was more than one type of angel in this group. There were unholy watcher angels or fallen angels and holy watcher angels. Knowing that watcher angels are here on earth with fallen ones as well, shows us the battle going on in the heavens between these angelic groups. Daniel realized their function but also realized their authority. He heeded the decree they made and the demand.

Daniel 4:17

17 This matter is by the decree of the watchers, and the demand by the word of the holy ones: to the intent that the living may know that the most High ruleth in the kingdom of men, and giveth it to whomsoever he will, and setteth up over it the basest of men.

Daniel 4:23

23 And whereas the king saw a watcher and an holy one coming down from heaven, and saying, Hew the tree down, and destroy it; yet leave the stump of the roots thereof in the earth, even with a band of iron and brass, in the tender grass of the field; and let it be wet with the dew of heaven, and let his portion be with the beasts of the field, till seven times pass over him;

These watcher angels were doing the job assigned to them as they came to the king, the one in authority. The book of Jubilee also confirms this title of watcher.

Jubilee 4:15,16   in the first week in the third year of this week, [395 A.M] and he called his name Mahalalel. And in the second week of the tenth jubilee [449-55 A.M.] Mahalalel took unto him to wife Dinah, the daughter of Barakiel the daughter of his father's brother, and she bare him a son in the third week in the sixth year, [461 A.M.] and he called his name Jared, for in his days the angels of the Lord descended on the earth, those who are named the Watchers, <u>that they should instruct the children of men, and that they should do 16 judgment and uprightness on the earth.</u>

Could the people of the Old Testament know

things about the spirit realm that we don't know or at the very least, that we have lost?

At this point, we have several facts we see in scripture backed up by other sources.

1. Satan fell because of iniquity.
2. Sin became manifest in the earth first, not in heaven.
3. The devil knew the seed of the woman would cause his demise.
4. Giants, who were also called watchers, mated with the women of the earth

Jewish Historian, Josephus

The foremost recognized authority and scribe, Josephus, wrote concerning the creation and offspring of angels and the women of the earth. He recognized the book of Enoch as a valid source of authority and saw no contradictions with other sources of information.

1. He concluded that watchers were upon the earth.

2. They mated with the women of the earth.
3. The offspring were gigantic in size and very brutal.
4. He also concluded that there were a few giants after the flood.
5. Those left were killed by David.

Ephesians 3:10

10 To the intent that now unto the principalities and powers in heavenly places might be known by the church the manifold wisdom of God,

Colossians 2:15 And having spoiled principalities and powers, he made a shew of them openly, triumphing over them in it.

As Jesus ascended, He gave gifts unto men. But before these spiritual authority gifts were left, he defeated every principality and power in the heavenly realm. He actually defeated Satan and fallen angels who had been given authority from men. This is why he came in the form of humanity, to take that authority back. I tell people the authority we have is proven authority. It is already exercised authority.

1. This defeat spoiled them.

2. This defeat was before all angels and

    heavenly beings.

3. This defeat was complete as He triumphed over them.

4. This defeat made them powerless in Christian lives.

These angelic beings are now defeated and await their judgment day! This is why all authority was given to Christ and now has been given to us.

1 Peter 3:22 Who is gone into heaven, and is on the right hand of God; angels and authorities and powers being made subject unto him.

Jesus the Victor

Jesus expects us to defeat every foe! He believes in you and me! But he also believes in His final authority even more. The outcome of this final authority is seen in scripture.

Colossians 2:13-15

13 And you, being dead in your sins and the uncircumcision of your flesh, hath he quickened together with him, having forgiven you all trespasses; 14 Blotting out the handwriting of ordinances that was against us, which was contrary to us, and took it out of the way, nailing it to his cross; 15 And having spoiled principalities and powers, he made a shew of them openly, triumphing over them in it.

Where did Jesus spoil these principalities and powers? While here on the earth and finally at the cross. Where did he triumph over them? He triumphed in the heavenly realm. But the key word in this scripture is the word 'spoil'. It does not mean something went bad or is rotten and now needs to be discarded. The word means 'to put off or strip'. It was a stripping away of authority and even ranking that occurred. It was like the ripping of a sergeant's stripe off his or her sleeve and busting them back to a private with no authority. In the military, this is done publicly so all know the person no longer carries the authority or weight of that position.

So it was when Jesus stripped the power of Satan. It says he made a "show" of them openly. The word for 'show' is word meaning more than even a public ceremony of stripping. The word means 'a triumphant procession'!

Imagine before all angels, both fallen and not, and all living creatures, the four beasts, the cherubim and seraphim this happened. The literal translation means 'to parade someone before others like a king who has won a battle and is leading his captors around so all know there is no more authority'. It is a complete and utter humiliation of their defeat and the victor's ultimate victory!

Greg Crawford

5

Daniel's Angelic Encounter

Now let's look at Daniel to a familiar passage of scripture and see the interaction of angels with humanity. This section is one we look at many times but seldom understand the full ramifications of what is happening in the unseen realm. We have heard the section in **Daniel 10** used to speak of prayer and fasting, angels fighting and holding fast in faith. But a closer look reveals many startling discoveries.

Daniel 10:1-9 (KJV 1900) — 1 In the third year of Cyrus king of Persia a thing was revealed unto Daniel, whose name was called Belteshazzar; and the thing was true, but the time appointed was long: and he understood the thing, and had understanding of the vision. 2 In those days I Daniel was mourning three full weeks. 3 I ate no pleasant bread, neither came flesh nor wine in my mouth, neither did I anoint myself at all, till three whole weeks were fulfilled. 4 And in the four and twentieth day of the first month, as I was by the side of the great river, which is Hiddekel; 5 Then I lifted up mine eyes, and looked, and behold a certain man clothed in linen, whose loins were girded with fine gold of Uphaz: 6 His body also was like the beryl, and his face as the appearance of lightning, and his eyes as lamps of fire, and his arms and his feet like in colour to polished brass, and the voice of his words like the voice of a multitude. 7 And I Daniel alone saw the vision: for the men that were with me saw not the vision; but a great quaking fell upon them, so that they fled to hide themselves. 8 Therefore I was left alone, and saw this great vision, and there remained no strength in me: for my comeliness was turned in me into corruption, and I retained no strength. 9 Yet heard I the voice of his words: and when I heard the voice of his words, then was I in a deep sleep on my face, and my face toward the ground.

Daniel had an angelic encounter because he was positioned before God. But it was more than an individual positioning; he had positioned himself for a nation! He had placed himself where he must have God's response not just for himself but for an entire people. This kind of motivation enables angelic visitation. God moves things at higher realms when our motive is not ourselves but for large groups of people. Many today want an angelic visitation so they cans say they had one. Daniel's did not start out seeking angels but seeking God!

Even though the verse says specifically that there were others around, only Daniel saw the vision of the angel. This could be because he was the only one with a prepared heart. It could be because the others did not have the same concerns towards the nation and the future as Daniel. It could also be that Daniel, as a statesman, had put himself in a position of "needing to know". I believe it's a combination of all these things. But Daniel is clear that he alone experienced this moment. I believe he writes it this way to eliminate confusion that others might say they saw it when in reality they did not. In **Daniel 10:1-7**, only Daniel saw the vision of the angel.

The pattern of angelic visitation in the Bible is not what we hear from so many today who claim an angel visited them. In the Bible, the first response was fear. The men with Daniel were quaking in fear and even ran and hid themselves. I believe Daniel would have as well but Daniel was frozen in the position to receive. A deep sleep fell on him. His senses were intact, his spirit alive to God. Daniel's encounter was first with the holiness angels bring. Some run from this holiness in terror like in this story. But because Daniel had prepared himself in fasting, not to change the mind of God, but to change himself, he saw himself no longer in the place of "honor" but that his honor was actually "corrupt" in comparison to the holiness that surrounded him.

Perhaps the reasons we don't have angelic visitations is all of these things spoken of until now. We are not seeking for others but for ourselves. We think we are positioned rightly when in reality we are not. We disregard the holiness of angels and instead of fear, we have pride because we treat what is holy as what is common.

Let's look at one last point in the text. He fell on his face on the ground. This is very key for the rest to unfold. He experienced a second and third heaven visitation. When we are receiving from God, we generally fall backward overwhelmed by how God has come towards us. We are strictly in a receiving mode. But when we fall forward, we are in a reverence mode. We are seeking God to speak whatever He desires and are not concerned about our personal need but God's intentions for humanity. Daniel fell face forward ready to hear whatever God would speak.

Daniel 10:12 Then said he unto me, Fear not, Daniel: for from the first day that thou didst set thine heart to understand, and to chasten thyself before thy God, thy words were heard, and I am come for thy words .

A key verse in this whole section of scripture is the above verse. The first thing the angel said to Daniel was "Fear not". It is the same greeting the angel gave Mary, the mother of Jesus and others. The angel knew Daniel was dealing with this emotion, probably by his reaction. The words following are so key to us mobilizing the unseen realm of angels. The angel in this verse gave Daniel an in-depth lesson into the government of angels, how they respond and what they respond to.

Let's look at the word meanings and begin to unpack the full meaning of this verse. The first thing said to Daniel stated how his heart was positioned. He "set" his heart towards a certain purpose to "understand". The word 'set' means 'to consecrate, to give or bestow'. But upon further investigation, the meaning of the word deepens. It means 'to place in a position by yielding that something could be produced'. It means 'to give your heart to another in such a fashion that nothing is held back and the other has the ability to do with your heart what they wish'! Now that's a definition!

This was not a preconceived idea of Daniel's. Nor was it a desire or his own selfish motive or intention in seeking God. He just placed himself in a path that said, "OK, God, here I am seeking to understand all that's going on so I will know how to respond the way You want me to respond. Anything You tell me will be fine!"

The understanding Daniel was after was not humanistic or might not even make sense for he desired some pretty radical direction and was determined to get it. That "understanding" was what the word really means to have discernment. 'To perceive by the spirit the real happenings and not only by observation'. You see, observation is what causes us to seek him and true spiritual understanding will cause us to rightly discern and lead us to places that may seem contrary to our natural mind.

This type of seeking and perceiving causes us to run out of words in our prayer life. It also causes us to see our own lack and need for God. Along the way, much of what we think we know begins to fade in comparison to what God knows. We come to the point of a divine exchange. Not my will but Yours. Not my desire but Yours. And eventually not my words, but Your words on this situation. We seem to think we know what needs said or done, but the ways of God are higher than ours. So are God's intentions and thoughts on a matter.

The angel basically told Daniel all this when he said to him I have come for YOUR words. He was really saying the divine exchange has occurred and you're not aware of it fully. For starter, the word – "words" is the Hebrew word for "Dabar". Dabar means 'to declare, promise, and command'. Daniel knew what God had promised but knowing it and declaring it are two different things. The word "Dabar" comes from a root word meaning 'to say what God says'. This root meaning carries even more impact when we understand it means 'to carry the breath of God in what is being said as if God Himself was speaking it'.

No wonder the angel came for his words. His words were the same words God would speak on the matter. They were not just mimicked words but words that actually had "Dabar" or the breath of God within them. Daniel was speaking as if God was speaking and the angels had no choice but to respond to his words. This type of speaking and declaring is what begins to move the angelic host as we have their attention.

The next thing the angel spoke of is how he heard what Daniel was saying. Now this is a fascinating verse. The angel was not just hearing some words coming from Daniel. Our mere words do not move angels as much as we would like to think. No, it takes something more than just praying some memorized or rehearsed type of prayer.

The word 'heard' in Hebrew is "shama" and it means 'to hear, listen and obey, to hear with attention and interest'. I wonder how much of what we say does not hold much interest for angels. But what becomes interesting is the makeup of the word "shama". It comes from two root words. The first part of the word means 'to perceive a message because of the sound of it'. Now that is real different. It is hearing because something has a life giving sound, a recognizable sound, a unique sound. The second part of the word means 'the news, fame and report attached to an individual generally about God'.

Now putting this together, Daniel was releasing a sound recognizable to the angels because it carried a dynamic with it. That dynamic was the breath of God. It also carried a report with it. I believe Daniel was speaking the report about who God was and what He had promised. But I also believe at the same time he was doing this that it also released a fame and report about himself that he did not even know was going on. That his deep association with God was placing him "in heavenly places" and created what I would call "a fame of association"!

Imagine us speaking like this! Not just some words to fill the air but words that released an atmosphere of honor to God. A place of dwelling is established, a hedge of protection. Angelic activity is in motion. Not by us begging, not by us praying, but by us decreeing with the breath of God and giving honor where honor is due so God would honor us. And God did just that. He honored Daniel with a visitation that we still look at today!

Next, the angel said he had not just appeared like we might think. The word "come" means 'to go in, entered in, enter in as entering a house'. It also means 'the entering in of God to: fight for His people, to meet with His people, to conduct business with His people'.

The angel was not just appearing but was on an assignment by God as His representative to do business on His behalf! Daniel had created an atmosphere, because of his heart, that allowed the angel to enter the atmosphere around him, so Kingdom business could be conducted.

Daniel 10:13 (KJV 1900) — 13 But the prince of the kingdom of Persia withstood me one and twenty days: but, lo, Michael, one of the chief princes, came to help me; and I remained there with the kings of Persia.

Now we begin to see the great war and conflict that angels are engaged into. The "prince of the kingdom of Persia" opposed this angel that spoke to him. This was not the king of Persia opposing but rather a fallen angel under Satan's control "of high rank, assigned by Satan, to Persia as his special area of activity". I find it amazing the angel did not draw back or stop forward motion because there was opposition. But when the angel heard Daniel's words, he had no choice no matter what was opposing to answer the call of those words!

We need to learn from this when God gives us a sure word to not draw back or abandon. We need to hold fast and allow the sound of that word to continue to draw us until all opposition is removed and we are standing at the point of fulfillment. So there was opposition but God always has a plan for what opposes. In this case, it was a second angel named Michael. It took two angels to open the way for Daniel to have an understanding of the situation. God will do whatever it takes for us and this case is no different.

The angel that spoke to Daniel was a messenger angel. This is an angel assigned to deliver a certain message from God. The angel that came and fought named Michael was a warring angel. He is called here, "one of the chief princes". The word 'chief' in Hebrew means 'first, foremost, beginnings or beginnings of time or creation'. He was an angel that saw the fall of the fallen ones and understood how to war against them.

He also was a prince. The word 'prince' in Hebrew means 'governor, leader, captain, official, military commander and general, overseer, ruler of rulers, one who would contend with power and reign'. So he was not a typical angel but a key angelic warrior called in at strategic times.

The first angel was holding ground but not breaking through. It took the second angel, Michael to war and open the way so the messenger angel could speak to Daniel. The period of time here is recorded as 21 days or from the moment Daniel started the journey through fasting, the messenger angel was deployed. Somewhere along the 21 day process Michael was deployed and the breakthrough came. It does not say they both fought for 21 days, only the messenger angel. I believe when Michael was deployed, it was a short to nonexistent amount of time that was needed to allow forward motion. Since Michael was the chief angel in this category, he held extreme authority over all other angels both fallen and not fallen.

I remember a time in my life that I went on a Daniel fast for 21 days. I had been confronting the Transcendental Meditation cult in my hometown. As a young Christian, I had very little understanding of angelic activity, I was basically naive. I knew angels existed but was clueless as to how they moved or what their assignments truly were.

I was in a prophetic office and was very much functioning in it. I would prophesy directive words almost weekly and was having visions and dreams on an ongoing basis. The church I was actively attending really did not know what to do with me and I got no real direction or development. But God would teach me and show me things. It was during one of these very intense battles I was doing in the spirit realm for the spiritual climate over our city that I was caught in a vision and saw for the first time the principality resting over our city.

The Lord told me to go to a certain hill and look over the cult campus in our city and He would show me something. When I got there, I suddenly had an open vision. By that, I mean it was like a part of the sky opened up and another realm was exposed to me through a portal. (A portal is a door or opening.) I was fully awake and was able to see both the natural world and then this portal taking about 30% of my vision as I peered into it.

I was able to see how demonic forces pushed against people with control and manipulation. I saw the principality was sitting on a false throne. He had the face of a gargoyle and a tarnished bent scepter in his hand. He would lower the scepter and point and the demonic forces would scurry through the city driving people to call on Hindu gods. The Lord showed me this in a moment of time but the overall vision lasted about 20 minutes or so.

When the vision was over, the Lord spoke to me and said that my prayer was not enough but He would assign an angel to fight for me. I could have this angel for three days and three days only, as he was needed for another battle. All I had to do was tell him what was needed and he would fight. I thought "Well, this is way cool!"

Then the Lord said to me the angel's name I am entrusting to you is Michael, he is my main warring angel. I was stunned. Is this the same Michael as in the scripture that Daniel encountered? The Lord answered "Yes"!

I was humbled and awed. And for the next three days, I commanded and decreed and the spiritual climate changed. This was the beginning of the shift of this cult activity in our region. To this day, I have not told this story to many as it is so holy a thing and others would so flippantly say, "oh yes, I commanded Michael...". When deep in my heart, I know they, in no way, had this kind of encounter by their conversation.

What started all of this in Daniel's life is that he had been studying the prophecy of Jeremiah concerning Israel's captivity. As you read what was prophesied, his heart was moved to the nation of Israel as a whole. This is where Daniel understood the promises of God, the words of God, and saw the prophecy that Jeremiah spoke as having the breath of God within it.

Daniel stood on these words and on other promises

of God to confess his and his people's sin and pray for the fulfillment of this promise. Daniel's words were based on God's words. He began to pray using God's word by the prophet Jeremiah as a basis for his words of prayer. This is what triggered the   angel.

Angels are not merely influenced by words, but more specifically by God's words. This is the language they understand. They know it is pure and holds God's intentions.

I believe that the words that Daniel spoke not only were reminders of what the prophet had already spoken, but I believe that Daniel was also able to bring the life of God fresh and anew into the existing words already declared. This breath of God carried with it a way to not only interact with heaven and Earth, but also moved the angelic host into action for heaven's sake upon the Earth.

In *Daniel 9:* **20-21** while Daniel was:

Speaking = "dabar" 'promise, pronouncing, declaring'

Praying = "Palal" 'to nudge the edge of the sword' – the word 'to impel'. 'To break or cut, to intervene, to fall prostrate, to take assessment, to judge'

Confessing = 'Praising, giving thanks, to confess the name of God, extol, acknowledge'

Presenting supplication= 'falling down prostrate-favor and grace'

Daniel was not doing motions but was in deep contemplation of God's promises. He was in a place of reflection and meditation. Daniel was taking assessment of the current condition and spiritual climate. He had decided to intervene by doing spiritual battle with the very words and breath that God had intended through the prophet Jeremiah. Daniel was also in the place of worshiping and calling out God's name. Daniel had not just postured himself with an attitude of his heart, but Daniel had found a place in God's grace and favor.

Psalm 103:20   Bless the LORD, ye his angels, that excel in strength, that do his commandments, hearkening unto the voice of his word.

You see, the voice that angels hearkened to is the voice of his word. The word 'voice' means 'the proclamation, same sound, noise, the calling aloud'. It is very similar to the calling forth of the birthing of creation. It is a voice that says everything must hearken to this decree that is being uttered. All the power of God, all the creative force and energy rallies around the fulfillment of what the voice is about to decree.

With the voice of God, decrees always are the "dabar" or the commanded speech and utterance that have the breath of God within it.

That word can be God's written word that is relevant to the current situation. That word can also be God's promise to us that the Holy Spirit gave us and that we now voice. That word can also be a prophetic utterance given by the Spirit.

Let's review Daniel's prayer with seven simple things that caused it to be greatly successful.

(1) Daniel's prayer was a *persistent,* no despairing interest (**Dan. 6:1-10**). In sixty-eight years of waiting, the prophet had not lost hope.

(2) He had *determination* (**vs. 3; Luke 9:51**).

(3) He showed *humility.* Note how he associated himself with his people in their sins. (**Luke 18:10-14; II Cor. 12:7**).

(4) He made *confession* (esp. **Dan 9:4, 5. Ps 32:5; 51:4; Jas 5:16**).

(5) He displayed *submission* (**Dan 9:14**) and engaged in

(6) *petition* and

(7) *intercession* (**Dan. 9, 10**)

Some of the things we do that move angels

1. **Our words**

   Daniel 10:12 (KJV 1900) — 12 Then said he unto me, Fear not, Daniel: for from the first day that thou didst set thine heart to understand, and to chasten thyself before thy God, thy words were heard, and I am come for thy words.

2. **Winning the Lost**

   Luke 15:7 (KJV 1900) — 7 I say unto you, that likewise joy shall be in heaven over one sinner that repenteth, more than over ninety and nine just persons, which need no repentance.

3. **Our worship**

   Angels always engage in our worship, especially if it is throne room worship or creative worship flowing from the heart. It is the great equalizer between heaven and Earth!

4. **Our declarations**

   We have seen how Daniel decreed and

angels went into motion.

5.   **When we are on assignment from God.**

Paul spoke of an angel standing beside him as he went to Rome.

Acts 27:23 (KJV 1900) — 23 For there stood by me this night the angel of God, whose I am, and whom I serve,

6.   **When we are in rough situations.**

Acts 5, Acts 12   Peter was in prison, but the angel of the Lord helped free him.

Psalm 34:7 The angel of the LORD encampeth round about them that fear him, and delivereth them.

7.   **At the time of calling.**

Moses at the burning bush   **Exodus 3, Acts 7:30**

8.   **When we receive doctrine.**

Acts 7:38 refers to when Moses received

doctrine or the law at Sinai.

9. During Prayer and Vision.

Acts 10:3 when we pray- Cornelius had a vision in the ninth hour, the hour of prayer, and an angel came to him.

6

Angels who are on Active Duty

Now we shall look at the different classifications of angels and what their functions truly are. Some of these will be new to us and some will be very familiar but maybe not classified as we have done here. Probably the most common misconception is that all angels function exactly the same. As we have seen from the short look in Daniel earlier in this book, we see different classifications with different functions. With these clearly understood, we can then begin to understand the importance of what God might be emphasizing. Under the function of being on active duty for God, there are three types of angelic beings: archangels, messenger angels and watcher angels. Each has a specific function as we are about to see.

Archangels

Let's begin by looking at archangels. Archangels are angels with the highest ranking. They are the Warring angels. Archangels are in charge of a host, which is mass of beings organized for war. Michael is the archangel we can identify. The name *Michael* means "who is like God?" and identifies the only one classified as an archangel in Scripture. Michael is the defender of Israel who wages war on behalf of Israel against Satan and his hordes in **Rev. 12:7–9.**

The mission of the archangel is protector of Israel and even more specifically, God's people who believe in Him. He is called "Michael your prince" in **Dan. 10:21.** Amazingly they did not recognize one angel like we would today but also recognized several archangels to say there were *chief princes* **(Dan. 10:13)**, of whom Michael was one, as the highest ranking angels of God. Not only did they understand or converse with many different archangels, but they knew a ranking existed as well!

Michael is also mentioned in these verses:

Daniel 10:13 (KJV 1900) — 13 But the prince of the kingdom of Persia withstood me one and twenty days: but, lo, Michael, one of the chief princes, came to help me; and I remained there with the kings of Persia

Daniel 12:1 *(KJV 1900) — 1 And at that time shall Michael stand up, the great prince which standeth for the children of thy people: and there shall be a time of trouble, such as never was since there was a nation even to that same time: and at that time thy* *people shall be delivered, every one that shall be found written in the book.*

Jude 9 (KJV 1900) — 9 Yet Michael the archangel, when contending with the devil he disputed about the body of Moses, durst not bring against him a railing accusation, but said, The Lord rebuke thee.

Michael also disputed with Satan about the body of Moses, but Michael refrained from judgment, leaving that to God. This shows his limited abilities but also reveals that even after death angels are still contending for us!

Jehovah's Witnesses and some Christians identify Michael as Christ; this view, however, would suggest Christ has less authority than Satan, which is indefensible. This has been easily shown in scripture as untrue. Michael is a created being and Christ is the Son of God.

Messenger Angels

Probably the most encountered category of angel is the messenger angel. Pastors in Africa who have almost weekly angelic encounters are having them with messenger angels.

They bring specific words from God to an individual. They also explain events, explain God's purposes, and are announcers. A good example of a messenger angel is with Mary, the mother of Jesus.

Luke 1:11–14 (KJV 1900) — *11 And there appeared unto him an angel of the Lord standing on the right side of the altar of incense. 12 And when Zacharias saw him, he was troubled, and fear fell upon him. 13 But the angel said unto him, Fear not, Zacharias: for thy prayer is heard; and thy wife Elisabeth shall bear thee a son, and thou shalt call his name John. 14 And thou shalt have joy and gladness; and many shall rejoice at his birth.*

The same pattern emerged; fear fell upon Zacharias as the angel began to speak to him. But the angel brought a specific message concerning the intentions of God for Elizabeth. Both Mary and Elizabeth had angelic visitations by messenger angels prior to conception. Both messages were very specific. During this same time, another messenger angel had spoken to Zacharias. It is not Gabriel as there is no mention of name. It appears from all the texts that they knew certain angels by name.

Luke 1:26-27 *And in the sixth month the angel Gabriel was sent from God unto a city of Galilee, named Nazareth , [27] To a virgin espoused to a man whose name was Joseph, of the house of David; and the virgin's name was Mary .*

Looking at the angelic visitation that Mary had, the angel began the encounter with Mary with a set message to be delivered. It told of "the intention of God". Gabriel is sent, which in Greek is the word *apostellos*, which means 'a sent one with a given message', 'a commander of an army or fleet of ships'. Gabriel was apostolically sent as he was also the chief messenger angel.

Luke 1:28–30 (KJV 1900) — 28 *And the angel came in unto her, and said, Hail, thou that art highly favoured, the Lord is with thee: blessed art thou among women.* **29** *And when she saw him, she was troubled at his saying, and cast in her mind what manner of salutation this should be.* **30** *And the angel said unto her, Fear not, Mary: for thou hast found favour with God.*

Again, fear is the reaction. Mary is troubled and her response is to doubt. The messenger angel repeated what was said in heaven about Mary. You see there are ongoing conversations in heaven concerning us. Messenger angels hear these conversations and then wait for God to speak to them to go release a certain part of what is said. Mary finding favor is a declaration of fact and has no speculation in it.

Luke 1:34–37 (KJV 1900) — *34 Then said Mary unto the angel, How shall this be, seeing I know not a man? 35 And the angel answered and said unto her, The Holy Ghost shall come upon thee, and the power of the Highest shall overshadow thee: therefore also that holy thing which shall be born of thee shall be called the Son of God. 36 And, behold, thy cousin Elisabeth, she hath also conceived a son in her old age: and this is the sixth month with her, who was called barren. 37 For with God nothing shall be impossible.*

Once again, the angel did not need to communicate with God about how to answer Mary's question but simply continued the conversation. You see God had already voiced in heaven His intentions and the angel simply repeated it. The angel, like any message from God we receive, had in this case, Mary's identity, purpose in life and final destiny in it. There is no speculation with a true message from God.

Luke 1:38 *(KJV 1900)* — *38 And Mary said, Behold the handmaid of the Lord; be it unto me according to thy word. And the angel departed from her.*

Mary received the angel's message as if it was God speaking to her. She yielded to the will of God through this angelic visitation. I believe this "word" given carried life with it and enabled Mary to conceive. The Bible says she conceived by the Holy Spirit. This "word" from the angel had the 'dabar' or the breath of God in it. This brought Mary into a spiritual place that the Holy Spirit could conceive through her. Remember the Holy Spirit had not been given to humanity yet, so Mary had to go to the place where the Holy Spirit was. The word carried her along on the breath of God!

Gabriel is the second name we recognize in scripture, yet there were other messenger angels as well. The name *Gabriel* means "man of God" or "God is strong." "Gabriel seems to be God's special messenger of His kingdom program in each of the times he appears in the Bible records. He reveals and interprets God's purpose and intentions concerning God and His kingdom to the prophets and people of Israel.

In a highly significant passage, Gabriel explained the events of the seventy weeks for Israel.

Daniel 9:21 *Yea, whiles I was speaking in prayer, even the man Gabriel, whom I had seen in the vision at the beginning, being caused to fly swiftly , touched me about the time of the evening oblation .*

In **Luke 1:26–27**, Gabriel told Mary that the One born to her would be great and rule on the throne of David. And in **Daniel 8:15–16**, Gabriel explained to Daniel the succeeding kingdoms of Medo-Persia and Greece as well as the untimely death of Alexander the Great.

Daniel 8:16–17 (KJV 1900) — *16 And I heard a man's voice between the banks of Ulai, which called, and said, Gabriel, make this man to understand the vision. 17 So he came near where I stood: and when he came, I was afraid, and fell upon my face: but he said unto me, Understand, O son of man: for at the time of the end shall be the vision.*

Watcher angels

Another category of angels is the watchers. These angels are assigned to the earth to watch over it from the beginning of time.

Daniel 4:17 (KJV)

17 This matter is by the decree of the watchers, and the demand by the word of the holy ones: to the intent that the living may know that the most High ruleth in the kingdom of men, and giveth it to whomsoever he will, and setteth up over it the basest of men.

Daniel states that this watcher angel made a decree concerning the Kingdom. He told how the Kingdom operates in the affairs of men. He went on to state in **verse 23** that the angel also spoke concerning what to do regarding governing the earth.

It appears these angels assigned as oversight of territories are already informed to the intentions of God concerning the earth. When they see things out of place, they already have the understanding to speak concerning these areas. Since speaking is the interaction with humanity, it is easy to confuse the different categories and think all angels are messenger type or in a single category. Angels speak based around their function or responsibility.

In the book of **Jubilees 4:15,** it tells of watcher angels who instructed men about judgment and uprightness on the earth.

Jubilees 4:15 *And in the second week of the tenth jubilee Mahalalel took unto him to wife Dînâh, the daughter of Barâkî'êl the daughter of his father's brother, and she bare him a son in the third week in the sixth year, and he called his name Jared; 9 for in his days the angels of the Lord descended on the earth, 1 those who are named the Watchers, 2 that they should instruct the children of men, 3 and that they should do judgment and uprightness on the earth.*

This gives specific and very detailed instruction. The book of **Enoch** in chapter **15**, refers to watcher angels. **Enoch 16:1** also refers to the watchers who fell at the beginning and the destruction they will experience.

Enoch 15:1 *And He answered and said to me, and I heard His voice: 'Fear not, Enoch, thou righteous man and scribe of righteousness: approach hither and hear my voice. 2. And go, say to the Watchers*

*of heaven, who have sent thee to intercede for
them: "You should intercede" for men, and not men
for you: 3. Wherefore have ye left the high, holy,
and eternal heaven, and lain with women, and
defiled yourselves with the daughters of men and
taken to yourselves wives, and done like the
children of earth, and begotten giants (as your)
sons? 4. And though ye were holy, spiritual, living
the eternal life, you have defiled yourselves with
the blood of women, and have begotten (children)
with the blood of flesh, and, as the children of men,
have lusted after flesh and blood as those [also] do
who die and perish. 5. Therefore have I given them
wives also that they might impregnate them, and
beget children by them, that thus nothing might be
wanting to them on earth. 6. But you were formerly
spiritual, living the eternal life, and immortal for
all generations of the world. 7. And therefore I have
not appointed wives for you; for as for the spiritual
ones of the heaven, in heaven is their dwelling. 8.
And now, the giants, who are produced from the
spirits and flesh, shall be called evil spirits upon
the earth, and on the earth shall be their dwelling.
9. Evil spirits have proceeded from their bodies;
because they are born from men, and from the holy
Watchers is their beginning and primal origin; they
shall be evil spirits on earth, and evil spirits shall
they be called. 10. As for the spirits of heaven, in
heaven shall be their dwelling, but as for the spirits*

of the earth which were born upon the earth, on the earth shall be their dwelling. 11. And the spirits of the giants afflict, oppress, destroy, attack, do battle, and work destruction on the earth, and cause trouble: they take no food, [but nevertheless hunger] and thirst, and cause offences. And these spirits shall rise up against the children of men and against the women, because they have proceeded from them.

Enoch 16:1 From the days of the slaughter and destruction and death [of the giants], from the souls of whose flesh the spirits, having gone forth, shall destroy without incurring judgment--thus shall they destroy until the day of the consummation, the great [judgment] in which the age shall be consummated, over the Watchers and the godless, yea, shall be wholly consummated." 2. And now as to the Watchers who have sent thee to intercede for them, who had been aforetime in heaven, (say to them): "You have been in heaven, but all the mysteries had not yet been revealed to you, and you knew worthless ones, and these in the hardness of your hearts you have made known to the women, and through these mysteries women and men work much evil on earth." 4. Say to them therefore: "You have no peace."'

Even Josephus, the foremost historian of the time, spoke of the common knowledge of Watchers. He alludes to them throughout his writings.

In **Dan 4:13**, Daniel saw a watcher angel.

Daniel 4:13-17 *I saw in the visions of my head upon my bed, and, behold, a watcher and an holy one came down from heaven ;* [14] *He cried aloud , and said thus, Hew down the tree, and cut off his branches, shake off his leaves, and scatter his fruit: let the beasts get away from under it, and the fowls from his branches :* [15] *Nevertheless leave the stump of his roots in the earth, even with a band of iron and brass, in the tender grass of the field; and let it be wet with the dew of heaven, and let his portion be with the beasts in the grass of the earth :* [16] *Let his heart be changed from man's, and let a beast's heart be given unto him; and let seven times pass over him.* [17] *This matter is by the decree of the watchers, and the demand by the word of the holy ones: to the intent that the living may know that the most High ruleth in the kingdom of men, and giveth it to* *whomsoever he will, and setteth up over it the basest of men.*

What we have covered here is not an all inclusive listing of watcher angels. This is just some of the main points. There are other areas in scripture where there are watcher angels but they are not specifically called "watcher" angels.

7

Angels Who Are Divine Attendants of God

Cherubim

Cherubim are not looked at as angels as we typically would understand them to be. Perhaps it is because cherubim are of the highest order or class, created with indescribable powers and beauty. Their main purpose and activity might simply be summarized in this way: they are proclaimers and protectors of God's glorious presence, His sovereignty, His glory, and His holiness.

They are first seen standing guard at the gate of the Garden of Eden, preventing sinful man from entering into what God deemed holy.

Genesis 3:24 *So he drove out the man; and he placed at the east of the garden of Eden cherubim, and a flaming sword which turned every way, to keep the way of the tree of life .*

They are also seen as the golden figures covering

the mercy seat above the ark in the Holy of Holies.

Exodus 25:17-22 *And thou shalt make a mercy seat of pure gold: two cubits and a half shall be the length thereof, and a cubit and a half the breadth thereof.* [18] *And thou shalt make two cherubim of gold; of beaten work shalt thou make them, in the two ends of the mercy seat.* [19] *And make one cherub on the one end, and the other cherub on the other end: even of the mercy seat shall ye make the cherubim on the two ends thereof.* [20] *And the cherubim shall stretch forth their wings on high, covering the mercy seat with their wings, and their faces shall look one to another; toward the mercy seat shall the faces of the cherubim be.* [21] *And thou shalt put the mercy seat above upon the ark; and in the ark thou shalt put the testimony that I shall give thee.* [22] *And there I will meet with thee, and I will commune with thee from above the mercy seat, from between the two cherubim which are upon the ark of the testimony, of all things which I will give thee in commandment unto the children of Israel .*

Wherever an emphasis on holiness is seen, you will find these angels standing watch. Unlike other categories of angels, these are mostly stationary. So not only are they the protector oversights of God's holiness but they are also attendants. This means they will react or do what is necessary to make sure God's holiness is not discredited or not reverenced. This is seen primarily in the Old Testament since in the New Testament, we are held personally accountable to maintain holiness.

A good example of this is seen when David brought in the ark and Uz'zah reached out to steady it. He was struck in half from the cherubim above the ark. These cherubim are only a representation of the actual ones guarding it. God placed them above the ark as a constant reminder of the holy cherubim who guard His holiness. It was actually the angels called cherubim that struck the man. The cherubim were on direct orders from God to protect what was holy and not to let anything defile it. It was not the act of touching, but the act of forgetting what was holy.

Cherubim have an extraordinary appearance with four faces — that of a man, lion, ox, and eagle. They had four wings unlike seraphim that have 6 wings. Another comparison feature is cherubim are seen below the sea of glass and seraphim are seen above the sea of glass. The sea of glass is the bottom of heaven's Throne or the floor of heaven. Moses peered upward with the seventy elders and saw the feet of God on the Throne. The sea of glass is the meeting place in heaven and is in constant motion reflecting the sounds and colors of the Throne Room. But what is important here is to understand that what is holy in heaven does not need protecting only that which is holy outside of heaven! Hence, cherubim are assigned outside the heavenly realm, while seraphim are seen in heaven.

In *Ezekiel 1*, we see they attended the glory of God, protecting it as it also contained God's presence. They were making sure as judgment was coming to a nation, that God's glory and presence would not be touched by it. Ezekiel was able to see these divine protectors and gave a report of seeing the likeness of and the appearance of both nine times associated around these cherubim. What Ezekiel saw was a representation of the presence or Spirit of God dwelling. 'The nine appearances of and nine likenesses of' are the fruit and gifts of the Spirit. These characteristics of Christ and sovereign out-workings or moving of the Spirit always have cherubim angels close by. They oversee and stand guard over these holy impartations of Christ and outward manifestations of His presence.

Ezekiel 10:15-17 *And the cherubim were lifted up. This is the living creature that I saw by the river of Chebar.* [16] *And when the cherubim went, the wheels went by them: and when the cherubim lifted up their wings to mount up from the earth, the same wheels also turned not from beside them.* [17] *When they stood, these stood; and when they were lifted up, these lifted up themselves also: for the spirit of the living creature was in them.*

We also see in **Ezekiel 10:15**, cherubim were actually orchestrating the movement of the wheels of God. These wheels are directly related to the movement of the throne. The simple act of the raising of the wings brought the wheels to attention. Upon further study, we can see a connection to the portal of God's Throne with the cherubim, four wheels, the eyes upon the wheels, and the activity that is being done. We cannot get into the details of this at this time as our focus in this writing is upon angels.

I will tell a personal story. Early on in my Christian walk, I started to be asked to speak at different smaller churches. On one occasion, I had a woman come up to me afterward and say "You need to know there were two large angels standing beside you today while you spoke. There was one on each side of you." I asked her what they were doing. "Standing at attention with swords at their sides" was her response. I was rather shocked by the whole conversation and at the time thought, 'well, that's pretty cool!' I did not have any understanding of their purpose but did wonder if every time a person is speaking before people whether angels are stationed there. Well this started happening to me over the next several years at different times and places. As I would finish speaking, people would come up and tell me the exact same vision. They all saw two angels standing on either side and at attention.

It wasn't until I did an in-depth study on angels years later that I realized these angels are probably there every time a person speaks. They are not typical angels, messenger angels, warrior angels, etc. These are definitely cherub type angels positioned by God to protect His presence, His sovereignty, His glory, and His holiness.

Seraphim

Just as we mentioned that cherubim are below the sea of glass, seraphim are above the sea of glass. Instead of four wings, they have six wings. The word '*seraphim*' means 'burning ones' and they are found surrounding the Throne of God. This is their place of function.

The main function of seraphim is to declare the holiness of God. This proclamation is generally seen as a threefold declaration of Holy, Holy, Holy. This translation is not only progressive in holiness but also is to recognize as both perfectly holy and extremely holy. Thus the emphasis reveals a depth of God that is truly seen around the Throne.

Isaiah 6:2–3 (KJV 1900) — *2 Above it stood the seraphim: each one had six wings; with twain he covered his face, and with twain he covered his feet, and with twain he did fly. 3 And one cried unto another, and said, Holy, holy, holy, is the LORD of hosts: The whole earth is full of his glory.*

Not only do they praise and proclaim the perfect holiness of God. The seraphim also express the holiness of God in that they proclaim that man must be cleansed of sin's moral defilement before he can stand before God and serve Him."

Isaiah 6:4–5 (KJV 1900) — *4 And the posts of the door moved at the voice of him that cried, and the house was filled with smoke. 5 Then said I, Woe is me! for I am undone; because I am a man of*

unclean lips, and I dwell in the midst of a people of unclean lips: for mine eyes have seen the King, the LORD *of hosts.*

These angels have the ability to take what is upon the altar of heaven and touch upon the lives of men. As we read further here in Isaiah, we can see they took a coal from the altar and touched the lips of Isaiah.

Isaiah 6:6–7 (KJV 1900) — *6 Then flew one of the seraphim unto me, having a live coal in his hand, which he had taken with the tongs from off the altar: 7 And he laid it upon my mouth, and said, Lo, this hath touched thy lips; and thine iniquity is taken away, and thy sin purged.*

Even though these angels are around the throne of God and are decreeing the holiness of God, they still use it only to take the coal from off the altar. In other words, they were not even allowed to have the chance of touching the altar itself even though they were assigned this unique place in heaven. It appears that this heavenly altar was to be reverenced and respected even by the angels that have the closest proximity to it. The angel took a live coal as opposed to a cold one that had burned out since it was no longer carrying the fire. How appropriate that a burning one takes a burning coal and touches the lips of Isaiah! Once again, the specific assignment is correlating to the specific function.

The coal and the touch from the altar had an effect upon Isaiah. It had the ability to purify his voice and what he would speak. But what is interesting is that Seraphim are around the throne of God. Isaiah had to have a Throne Room experience to be able to be purged in such a fashion. The angel did not come to the Earth and touch his lips. Isaiah entered into the Throne Room and was cleansed in the heavenly realm.

The word *'lips'* in Hebrew means 'language'.

The coal was actually touching the language of Isaiah. Not only was Isaiah's lips cleansed, but so was his iniquity, or twisted thinking and lawlessness. His sins were reconciled and he was placed in right standing before God. I must point out here that the angel did not do the cleansing action but it was a coal from off the altar that was used to perform this. The angel is only the instrument that God used to carry the coal to touch Isaiah.

This passage in Isaiah is the only passage where seraphim are listed in the Bible. There is very little that refers to them in other sections of Scripture as well. But with the descriptions that we see and the function that we see here, we can come to the conclusion that most Throne Room visitations have some form of seraphim activity surrounding them. When I have had a Throne Room visitation in the past, it has caused me to look at my own life and see my greater need of God. I have also been confronted with the things in my life that need to change. I believe that in some of these aspects, seraphim were also involved in that activity, yet I did not realize it.

8

Angelic Governmental Structure

Up to this point, we've been given a basic understanding of angelic activity, functions and categories. We have seen some patterns emerge in Scripture and also the function of angels in different dynamics interacting with humanity upon the earth. Now we will look further into this angelic structure that God designed and see that it is a reflection of God's government that He wants the Church, had always planned for the Church, to function in.

What I'm about to share is the revelation the Lord has given to me concerning angelic government. For starters, I will say that angels are willing to hold what men refuse to hold. I believe it is the role of God's fivefold ministry government to hold and function in some ways how the angelic host functions. We should be doing spiritual warfare, we should be messengers of God, we should be declaring the holiness of God and protecting it, and we should be burning ones. All of the dynamics that we have seen describing angels are actually somewhat a description of what God would want out of His fivefold ministers and leaders.

103

In the Old Testament, angels helped govern the spiritual condition but they were limited because of man's free will operating in opposition to them. They have been given a measure of authority but not full authority. This is unlike man who has been given full authority, which is either rightly exercising it or delegating it, unfortunately, to satanic influences. As we see how angels operated in the Old Testament trying to bring the intentions of God, so should we, His fivefold ministers and leaders today.

In the New Testament, man's will is more aligned because of the Holy Spirit and not in so much direct opposition to what and how God desires to govern. The Holy Spirit has become a great teacher, comforter, instructor, and revealer. The Holy Spirit's role has replaced much of what angelic messengers in the Old Testament would do. Perhaps this is why we do not have so many angelic encounters as they did in the Old Testament. But I do believe there is a balance for angelic activity in our life, as long as our life is in balance with the Holy Spirit. If we are more focused on angelic activity surrounding us than on the Holy Spirit, then we are out of balance and in danger of worshiping angels.

What we have seen so far is that angels are given angels under them to command. We see that there are chief angels as well as other angels. This points to a structure or a way of governing that God has put into place. Once again, we see that God has an overall structure that He wants us to follow and the pattern is repeated through families, the Church and fivefold ministries, and even into angelic functions.

Revelation 12:7-8 And there was war in heaven: Michael and his angels fought against the dragon; and the dragon fought and his angels, 8 And prevailed not; neither was their place found any more in heaven.

But we also see that angels take and give orders. We see that there are other angels submitted one to another and working in harmony to bring the intentions of God upon the Earth. We have seen that there are angels overseeing other angels and even waiting for them to complete their assignment before their own assignment can take hold. We have also seen that there is no insubordination or unwillingness to perform certain assignments given. We see that once an assignment was given to an angel, they held fast until it was completed.

These things are all governmental or show governmental structuring. If angels are in a form of governmental structure, then so should we be. I believe we are falling far short as the Church or true ecclesia of God, in moving in full authority that we have been entrusted with. We can see from the previous paragraph, that many of those things that angels do, we do not do or fall short of completing.

Governmental positioning

There is a tremendous parallel of the different groups of angels and the government of God. Upon aligning them side by side, we begin to see just how much God is a God of order and structure. The longer I study all kinds of different topics the more I see you just cannot escape a governing body being established as oversight for the Body of Christ.

In **Ephesians 4**, we see there is a government that God has set up of the fivefold ministries. There are five distinct gifts with the reality of a fourfold function. As you look at the angelic structures, we also see the same pattern emerging of five distinct giftings. If we begin to parallel these, they look something like this:

Apostles – Archangels

- Both are warriors and conquerors.
- Both have strategic assignments.
- Both oversee and direct others.

Prophets – Messenger angels

- Both have God's heart and intention.
- Both have foreknowledge.
- Both bring a specific message.
- Both bring a message that may not be understood.

Pastors – Watcher Angels

- Both are assigned to watch over Earth and humanity.
- Both are given specific territory.
- Both are not transient but are more resident.

Teachers – Cherubim

- Both are proclaimers.
- Both are protectors of the truth.
- Both are protectors of God's holiness.
- Both are called to protect what is precious to God.

Evangelists - Seraphim

- Both are trying to bring men into the holiness of God.
- Both look at how sin holds back man's approach to God.
- Both take coals from the altar to touch the lips and heart of men.

Now I know that these things seem hard to receive but there are distinct similarities. There is also a governmental structure with angels. Each one is staying in their function and assignment. And each one allows others to function in their assignment.

I believe that there are primary corresponding angels to each office working alongside God's government. I also believe these are untapped resources to help us align with heaven for a greater impact.

Let's look further into **Enoch 40:9** for four governmental functions that angels have been assigned to do. Interestingly enough, they lineup with the descriptions that we've seen in Scripture and also with the fivefold governmental functions.

1. The first that is mentioned is Michael the Archangel. It is said that he is merciful and has long-suffering. That he is a warring angel. This is very much a description of how all apostles must function in this day.

2. The second angel mentioned is Raphael. Raphael was appointed over all disease and the wounds of the children of men. Once again, this is the role of a pastor and teacher. Healing the wounds through great love and instructing in the process.

3. The third is Gabriel. He is said to have all power over all messenger angels. He brings the intentions of God into the hearts of men. As a messenger angel, he is said to have foreknowledge concerning God's intentions as events unfold. This is very much like the office of a prophet.

4. Finally, the fourth angel listed in Enoch is Phanuel. This angel had oversight concerning repentance and was to bring a hope to those who

would inherit eternal life. This definitely is an Evangelist.

Looking at how angels war

2 Corinthians 10:4-6

⁴ (For the weapons of our warfare are not carnal, but mighty through God to the pulling down of strong holds ;) ⁵ Casting down imaginations, and every high thing that exalteth itself against the knowledge of God, and bringing into captivity every thought to the obedience of Christ; ⁶ And having in a readiness to revenge all disobedience, when your obedience is fulfilled.

Something we need to be aware of is that as we are engaged in spiritual warfare, so are angelic forces that have been assigned to help us contend. I believe that they use some of the same weapons that we do as they come alongside us to bring the intentions of God into the earth. In the New Testament, the word *'weapons'* is always used in the plural form. This means there are multiple types of weapons or tools or implements used in spiritual warfare.

In the above verse, Paul's reference here is to strongholds, which requires a siege engine to tear down or attack. (A siege engine required multiple people involved so a stronghold could be taken). Since our approach is spiritual and the world's approach is very different, let's look at how the world would approach the weapons that they would use in combating difficult situations.

The weapons of the world are:

1.   learning,
2.   personal influence,
3.   impressive credentials **1 Cor. 1:26**
4.   rhetorical polish **1 Cor. 2:1**

The weapons Paul used were the proclaimed Word of God and prayer (**Eph. 6:17-18**), these were weapons with divine power. In dependence on God (**1 Cor. 2:4-5**) these weapons, frail by worldly standards, are able to demolish the arguments and every pretension of the Gospel's foes. Neither the god of this Age nor his henchmen could oppose the knowledge (or power) of God on which Paul relied. No thought, including those of his opponents, is beyond the reach of the One who "catches the wise in their craftiness" and "knows that the thoughts of the wise are futile". (**1 Cor. 3:19-20; Job 5:13; Ps. 94:11**)

Ephesians 6:16-18

16 Above all, taking the shield of faith, wherewith ye shall be able to quench all the fiery darts of the wicked. 17 And take the helmet of salvation, and the sword of the Spirit, which is

the word of God : 18 Praying always with all prayer and supplication in the Spirit, and watching thereunto with all perseverance and supplication for all saints ;

Paul's weapons were the word of God and prayer. The meaning of "word" is the Greek word *'Rhema'*. *Rhema* means that which is or has been uttered by the living voice, thing spoken, word. Any sound produced by the voice and having definite meaning. It comes from a root word which means 'a command that has been poured out'! It can also mean 'an announcement' or even 'a treaty or covenant that has been established'. Our main overall weapon is the Word of God. I also believe that the Word of God is also the angels main weapon by which they fight and battle. After all, all things that they do have been given by God's voice spoken to them and commanded to them. Think how powerful it is that not only are we voicing the Word of God as we battle, but also angels are moving on the Word of command of God as well.

2 Corinthians 6:7

7 By the <u>word of truth</u>, by the power of God, by the armour of righteousness on the right hand and on the left,

Ephesians 3:3

3 How that by revelation he made known unto me the mystery; (as I wrote afore in few words,

The word 'revelation' means 'a laying bare, making naked, a disclosure of truth, by instruction'. It is always focused on concerning things before unknown. It is used 'of events by which things or states or persons hitherto withdrawn from view are made visible now'. It really means 'a manifestation or the bringing into appearance something once not known'.

As we go to war, most of the time we speak what we say based on past words God has spoken to us. This is the *logos* of God and not the *rhema*. What we really need is to base our present warfare on God's current words that are fresh to us which is God's *rhema* word. As angels move on what God has said and what we are declaring, when new revelation comes, fewer angels are released until more people confess the same thing. That is why when new revelation comes, it is so hard to see it manifest.... There is a great war in the heavens over the revealed Word of God.

As the new revelation is starting to take more ground, it creates more spiritual confrontation. We are attacked as the ones voicing the revelation, and forget that angels are wrestling to perform God's intentions concerning it. Once new revelation takes hold and becomes commonplace, men contend and fight for it and angelic hosts are released from that assignment to fight for the next level of new revelation.

Romans 6:13 *Neither yield ye your members as instruments of unrighteousness unto sin: but yield yourselves unto God, as those that are alive from the dead, and your members as instruments of righteousness unto God.*

What makes the angelic host seem to be so effective in what they do is the right standing that they have with God. They are holy angels sent to do a holy assignment for a holy God. We, as members of the Body of Christ, also have a weapon of our lives that are made righteous in Christ Jesus. Our life can literally be a weapon that God can use.

Romans 13:12

[12] *The night is far spent, the day is at hand: let us therefore cast off the works of darkness, and let us put on the armour of light.*

There are other writings that teach us about angels as well. One of these writings is called the War Scrolls. The War Scrolls speak of all known battles with Sons of Light and Sons of Darkness. The War Scrolls speak of trumpets sounding with words written upon them. It also talks about swords that have the Word of God written upon them. Without the Word of God written upon the sword, the sword would be seen as ineffective and useless in the battle.

Although the war talked about in the War Scroll is said to extend over forty years, the writer of the Scroll was particularly concerned with the details of the very final day of battle. After six bloody engagements during this last battle, the Sons of Light and Sons of Darkness are deadlocked in a 3-3 tie. In the seventh and final confrontation, "the great hand of God shall overcome Belial and all the angels of his dominion, and all men of his forces shall be destroyed forever"

(1QM 1:14-15).

In three lots the Sons of Light shall stand firm so as to strike a blow at wickedness, and in three the army of Belial shall strengthen themselves so as to force the retreat of the forces of Light. And when the banners of the infantry cause their hearts to melt, then the strength of God will strengthen the hearts of the Sons of Light. In the seventh lot: the great hand of God shall overcome Belial and all the angels of his dominion, and all the men of his forces shall be destroyed forever.

Something that is very interesting in the War Scroll, page 7, was that upon the soldiers' shields are written the four angels that we have seen earlier in **Enoch 40:9**. It was symbolic that they were taking angelic hosts of all functions into battle with them.

On page 9 of the War Scrolls, we see angels condemn the earthly adversaries that are fallen watcher angels. Interesting in this writing of the battles between light and darkness, that watcher angels are brought up, once again, in a different historical document.

We have seen the pattern that angels move on the words of God, *DABAR*. These words are either spoken by Him or spoken by us. Now let us turn back to look at Daniel, once again, with his encounter in **Daniel 10**. We know that the angel came for Daniel's words. What Daniel had spoken released a great spiritual battle in the heavens.

Daniel 10:13 *But the prince of the kingdom of Persia <u>withstood</u> me one and twenty days: but, lo, Michael, one of the chief princes, came to <u>help</u> me; and I remained there with the kings of Persia.*

117

'*Withstood*' means 'to remain, endure, to take a stand' (attitude).

The word '*help*' means 'support', and refers to military assistance; "*Azar*" in Hebrew is put with other names to refer to the divine. *Azarel* ("God has helped"), *Azriel* (" My help is God"), *Azariah* ("The Lord has helped") and *Ezra* ("help," but possibly from a form meaning "the Lord helps"), and *Ebenezer* ("stone of help").

This means 'a divine assistance by military action'.

Daniel 10:20 *Then said he, Knowest thou wherefore I come unto thee? and now will I return to fight with the prince of Persia: and when I am gone forth, lo, the prince of Grecia shall come .*

From this, we see that once the angel removes himself from his position, another principality will have to be confronted. God, in the Old Testament, not only fought "in the Spirit" but used angels to bring death, He used nature's elements to work out His intentions. But what God uses to fight with has to be holy and set apart.

Numbers 21:14 *Wherefore it is said in the book of the wars of the LORD, What he did in the Red sea, and in the brooks of Arnon,*

This Book of Wars is only mentioned once and is a lost book. However, not every battle was a war wherein everything in the captured city was devoted to destruction. Further, many of Israel's wars were civil wars between the tribes and even selfish wars of aggression. Perhaps this book will be found one day and we will see more glimpses into the battles that angelic hosts fight alongside men.

Greg Crawford

9

Ministry of Angels

Angels have two spheres they minister in or operate in: Heaven and Earth. Some are assigned only to one sphere. So now, let's look at the different placements in Heaven or in Earth.

Heavenly Ministry

Ministry to God. The cherubim have a ministry to God in defending the holiness of God; Seraphim have a ministry to God in surrounding the Throne of God as they attend to His holiness.

Ministry to Christ. Angels have a significant ministry to Christ from before His birth until His Second Advent. The fact that angels have this important ministry to Christ also emphasizes His deity; just as the angelic beings surround the Throne of the Father, so the angels attend to God the Son.

> (1) Angels predicted His birth (**Luke 1:26–38**). Gabriel came to Mary explaining that her child would be called "Son of the Most High," who would also rule on the throne

of David, His father, having an eternal kingdom.

(2) Angels protected Him in infancy (**Matt. 2:13**). An angel warned Joseph of Herod's intention and told Joseph to flee to Egypt until the death of Herod. An angel also instructed Joseph when it was safe to return to the land of Israel (**Matt. 2:20**).

(3) Angels ministered to Him after the temptation (**Matt. 4:11**). The ministry probably included encouragement following the exhaustion of forty days of temptation, as well as supplying him with food as an angel did for Elijah (**1 Kings 19:5–7**).

(4) Angels strengthened Him at Gethsemane (**Luke 22:43**). Just as Christ had a spiritual battle with Satan at His temptation, so Christ had a spiritual battle at Gethsemane concerning the cross. Angels strengthened Him as He wrestled in prayer in anticipation of His crucifixion.

(5) Angels announced His resurrection (**Matt. 28:5–7; Mark 16:6–7; Luke 24:4–7; John 20:12–13**). The angels invited the women to enter the empty tomb to see the

empty wrappings that they might be certain of the resurrection and proclaim it to the world. The angels reminded the women of Jesus' earlier promise that He would rise on the third day.

(6) Angels attended His ascension (**Acts 1:10**). As angels surround the throne of the Father, so angels attended the triumphal ascension of the Son into glory and reminded the onlookers of Jesus' future triumphant return.

(7) Angels will attend His Second Coming (**Matt. 25:31**). Angels will prepare the world for the return of the Son by regathering Israel to the land preparatory for their Messiah's return and rule (**Matt. 24:31**). As God, the Son, returns to earth, He will be attended by a host of angels, adding to the splendor and glory of His triumphal return (**Matt. 25:31**).

Psalm 103:20-21

²⁰ *Bless the LORD, ye his angels, that excel in strength, that do his commandments, hearkening*

unto the voice of his word. ²¹ *Bless ye the LORD, all ye his hosts; ye ministers of his, that do his pleasure.*

Angels not only worship God but do His commandments, hear His voice and minister His pleasure. If angels do this, then we are expected to do the same things!

Earthly Ministry

Ministry to believers. Angels are termed "ministering spirits" in **Hebrews 1:14**. The Greek term for *ministering (leitourgika)* does not convey the idea of slavery but of official functioning. They have been duly commissioned and sent forth with the responsibility of aiding believers. The following responsibilities are carried out in angels' ministry to believers.

(1) Physical protection. David experienced physical protection by the angel when he was forced to flee to the Philistines (**Ps. 34:7**). Angels may frustrate the plans of the enemies of God's people (**Ps. 35:5**) Let the angel of the Lord chase them. Angels protect from physical harm those that seek refuge in the Lord (**Ps. 91:11–13**). They released the apostles

from prison (**Acts 5:19**) and Peter from prison (**Acts 12:7–11**).

Matthew 18:10 *Take heed that ye despise not one of these little ones; for I say unto you, That in heaven their angels do always behold the face of my Father which is in heaven.*

Psalm 34:7 *The angel of the LORD encampeth round about them that fear him, and delivereth them.*

(2) <u>Physical provision</u>. An angel brought physical nourishment for Elijah when he was weakened from a lengthy journey (**1 Kings 19:5–7**).

(3) <u>Encouragement</u>. During the storm at sea, an angel encouraged Paul, reminding him he would arrive safely to Rome to bear witness for Christ (**Acts 27:23–25**). This angel knew Paul's assignment and was there to encourage him to not lose track of that assignment.

(4) <u>Direction</u>. An angel gave general direction to Philip to go south (**Acts 8:26)** but the actual

direction to witness to the Ethiopian eunuch was given by the Spirit speaking to him, (**Verse 29**). This was the specific action to take. An angel arranged the meeting of Cornelius and Peter that brought the Gentiles into acceptance in the believing community   (**Acts 10:3, 22**).

(5) <u>Assist in answers to prayer</u>. Daniel's prayer was explained by the angel (**Dan. 9:20–27; 10:10–12:13**). There seems to be a relationship between the prayer for Peter's release from prison and the angel releasing him (**Acts 12:1–11**). The angel only did for Peter what he could not do for himself! The angel knew what Peter could do and expected him to contribute! God can only do what is impossible if we do what is possible. Prayer does not release Peter but prayer released the angel to release Peter! The people prayed and released the intentions of God. The angel carried out the intentions of God.

(6) <u>Carry believers home.</u>   **Luke 16:22** describes the death of Lazarus and the angels carrying him to Abraham's bosom. This may be the way God causes all His dying saints to be "absent from the body...at home with the Lord."

Relationship to unbelievers. Angels have been

and will be involved in meting out judgment on unbelievers. Angels announced the coming destruction of Sodom because of the people's sin (**Gen. 19:12–13**); prior to the climactic bowl judgments, angels will announce the destruction of the world powers along with those that worshiped the beast (**Rev. 14:4, 7–9, 15, 17, 18**). Angels are seen judging the people of Jerusalem for their idolatry (**Ezek. 9:1–11**); an angel struck Herod Agrippa I for his blasphemy so that he died (**Acts 12:23**). Angels will also be instrumental in judgment at the end of the age when they cast unbelievers into the furnace of fire (**Matt. 13:39–42**); angels will sound the trumpet judgments during the Tribulation (**Rev. 8:2–12; 9:1, 13; 11:15**); angels pour out the bowl judgments upon the earth (**Rev. 16:2–17**).

As we can see from this short teaching on angels, there is much we do not understand and still make assumptions. It is my prayer that we become more tuned into the unseen and eternal realm and understand how it functions by being governmentally aligned with heaven, and that we could learn from this function as well.

Even at the time of this writing, I experienced another angelic visitation. It occurred in a worship meeting at our ministry. As the prophetic creative flow of worship brought us to a holy place, angelic voices could be heard singing for almost 25 minutes with the worship instruments. Many heard it and testified of it. It touched some who were left in tears from hearing such beauty. Others on the live stream said it was crystal clear. I wondered, could this have come about because I was writing on the subject and was more open to the possibility of angelic visitation? We need to realize that God has placed angels not for our entertainment but to truly help us contend!

ABOUT THE AUTHOR

Greg Crawford has been active in ministry for over 30 years serving in almost every type of leadership role. He is the founder of Jubilee International Ministries which recently relocated to Des Moines, Iowa. He and his wife, Julie, have also co-labored in founding Jubilee School of Ministry and Jubilee International School of Ministry which now has 40+ schools in developing nations. The International School network graduates roughly 5,000 students yearly. They have grown the network of schools to stand on their own within their nation without ongoing support from the United States. Jubilee School of Ministry in the USA has international graduates who have established schools and works in many nations of the world as well. Many have planted churches orphanages, and are involved in high places of influence in governments. Today Jubilee School of Ministry is no longer a class room but is an online school of ministry training with over 350 hours of online instruction.

Apostle Crawford or APG as he is know by, has traveled on numerous international trips, leading teams into nations conducting leadership conferences. He has worked in Cote D Vire, Nigeria, South Africa, Zambia, and Indonesia. Many of the nations have had reoccurring trips as he has taken teams of ministers with him. He laid the ground work for the apostolic reformation in Nigeria with close to 12 trips to this nation alone, teaching thousands of leaders on team ministry and the apostolic for the first time. With close to 50 ministers ordained under them in the United States, they also provide counsel and insight, helping many church leaders today.

Apostle Crawford has become a spiritual father to many and has a desire to see the generations running together as one voice. He has labored to see the Kingdom expression of reformation and awakening come by travels in Iowa and the United States to help bring this into existence. He is best known for his revelatory teaching style and has a unique and powerful ministry of laying on of hands for impartation. He carries a deep message that release the breath of God to confront the hearts of believers. This has opened the door for him to speak at many national conferences. The revelatory dynamic has enabled him to write over 10 books, write close to 300 hours of classes, some taught by secular colleges, and to send out a bi-monthly teaching through email. His teachings can be found on many websites and have been the lead feature article on Identity Network a leading prophetic voice in America with a web base following of close to 350,000.

He holds a PHD of Ministry which he received Magna Suma Cum Laude. He is ordained with Jim Hodges' Federation of Ministries and Churches International and is in relationship with several well know national voices. Currently he is overseeing The BASE, a ministry located in Des Moines to bring awakening and reformation to the church and culture. The forerunner ministry of the BASE has creative spontaneous worship created in the moment, gift and call devolvement, investment by spiritual fathering, and revelatory instruction with opportunity. More information can be found at the ministry website **www.thebaseiowa.org**

For More information contact

"The Base"

Des Moines, Iowa

www.thebaseiowa.org

Made in the USA
Monee, IL
11 February 2020